AIM HIGH, LITTLE GIANT, AIM HIGH!

Bobbito García

AIM HIGH, LITTLE GIANT, AIM HIGH!
Written & Art Directed by Bobbito García
Copyright © 2022 by Bobbito García
Cover design by Estefanía Rivera Cortés
Cover copyright © 2022 by Estefanía Rivera Cortés, Bobbito García & Little Giants Giant Shorties
Illustrated by Estefanía Rivera Cortés
Illustration Copyright © 2022 Estefanía Rivera Cortés, Bobbito García & Little Giants Giant Shorties
Layout & Typesetting by Ivan Rivera
Published by LGGS, LLC dba Little Giants Giant Shorties
Printed in China

First Edition: 2022

Bobbito García
www.koolboblove.com
@koolboblove

Estefanía Rivera Cortés
www.estefaniariveracortes.com

Little Giants Giant Shorties
www.wearelittlegiants.com
@wearelittlegiants.com

ISBN: 978-0-9985322-7-1

This book is dedicated to all the children worldwide who play ball outdoors, keeping the sport pure as can be, and to their parents, caretakers and community who provide the safe space for these little giants to "aim high!"

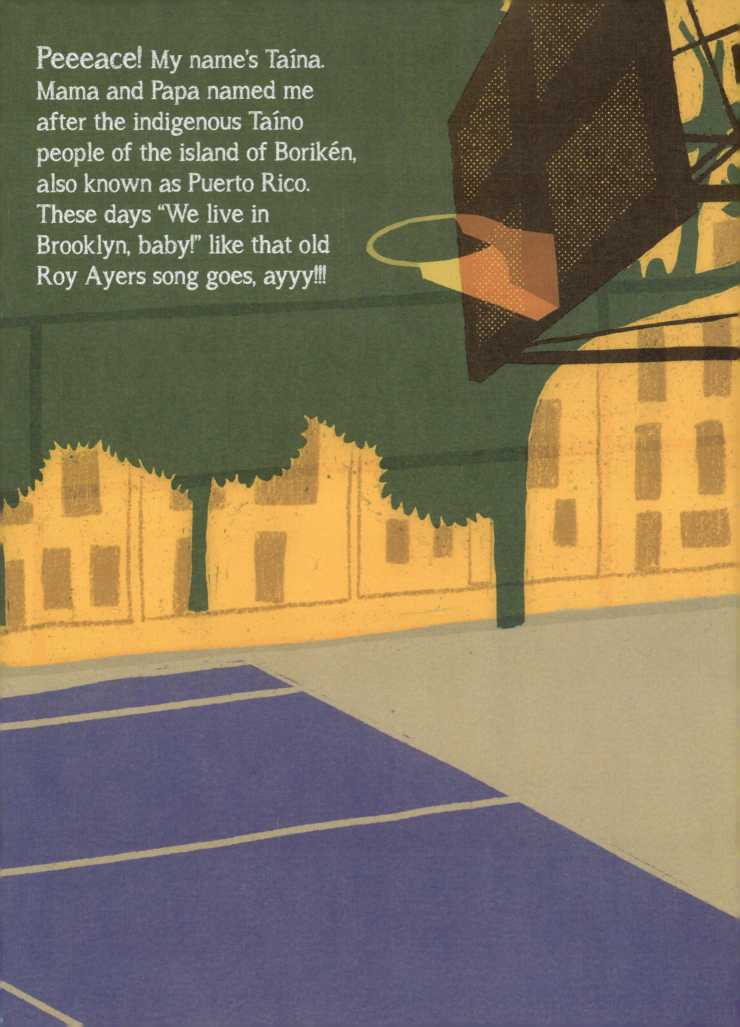

Peeeace! My name's Taína. Mama and Papa named me after the indigenous Taíno people of the island of Borikén, also known as Puerto Rico. These days "We live in Brooklyn, baby!" like that old Roy Ayers song goes, ayyy!!!

I'm amped up because Papa is doing a b-ball clinic at the biddy court. I prefer the rims there because I'm not confident shooting on a regulation 10-foot basket. With the target at eight feet, I can develop solid shooting form without straining myself.

I think Papa also digs being able to dunk on the kiddie court, because he's never done that in a real game. My father has negative ups, ha!

"Taína, wait, I have something for you!" Baba Kyle always sees us walking out of our building from the top step of his brownstone stoop. "Catch..."

...and with the accuracy of a Trae Young three-pointer from 35 feet, the kindest neighbor on our block throws me a guanabana (some call it soursop) that lands directly in my hands. "Gracias, Baba Kyle! We'll add this to a green smoothie later. Yum!"

I see Ibrahim and greet him respectfully in Arabic, "As-salamu 'alaikum, Ibrahim!" He wishes me peace in return, "Wa-'alaikum as-salaam, Taína. Can I run, too?"

"I'll ask Papa, but you've got a few years on me—why would you want to learn the basics?"

"Yeah, nah—I've been playing since I was your age, but no one's ever taught me the fundamentals..."

Ibrahim grabs my ball and takes a hop step towards the rim, jumping awkwardly off both feet with his right arm cocked back in position to dunk...except he's left-handed. The ball pings off the bottom of the iron and bops him in the forehead, then by accident, bounces off the backboard and nestles into the hole for two!

"There's a game called H.O.R.S.E. where if a player makes a trick shot, the next participant attempts the same shot. On a miss, they get a letter. I think you would be great at it, Ibrahim!"

Time for the clinic! Papa directs me and my homies Theophilus, Ireyna, Mamushi, and Ibrahim to do a breathing exercise before we even stretch. I always want to help, so today, he asks me to lead...

"Okay, everyone, deep breath in...hold for four seconds... breath out, hold for four seconds, now repeat..."

I can feel myself becoming more relaxed. Anytime Mama sees me get angry, or Papa notices I'm frustrated with my shot, they encourage me to use this as a calming strategy. It doesn't always work, but maybe if I keep practicing, I'll get better at it!

Mama has told me I have a growth mindset. She's great at encouraging my effort, no matter the result. I love her so much.

Papa then asks us to close our eyes and be quiet for two minutes. I can be super fidgety, so this will be hard!

"I don't know if I can do it, Papa." He responds, "You won't know if you don't try."

So, I close my eyes, and my mind travels. I imagine strokes of brilliant primary colors from art class. I can visualize a platypus...performing yo-yo tricks on his bill?

"Keep your eyes closed, Taína. 30 more seconds..."

"Okay, open them. Let's each take a turn sharing what we heard..."

Theophilus, Mamushi, and Ibrahim heard a plane, an ambulance siren, and young children laughing on the swings. Papa heard a player dribbling a couple of blocks away. If a doctor took an x-ray of Papa's brain, it would have the same grooves and panels as an actual basketball!!

"I heard the wind blow, and the call of a red-tailed hawk landing on the tree branch above us. Ireyna, what did you hear?"

"All I could hear was my foot tapping from being so antsy to play, ha! So...when do we finally get to touch a rock?"

Something feels off today. Papa said Theophilus, Mamushi, Ireyna, and Ibrahim's parents all shared that they couldn't attend the clinic this week. We head out to the park to play ball regardless, but Baba Kyle isn't on his stoop watching over the block like he usually is. The sidewalks...are empty.

We arrive at the court, and there's a big sign on the fence stating that everyone must stay socially distanced and exercise alone. I hear Papa gasp, like I had never heard before. I look up at the backboards, and...the rims were taken down. On every court.

I grab Papa's hand and give him a hug.

He probably feels the same way I did when the charger broke on my tablet. I had to be off screens for a week! Maybe it's like the time I was eating yummy BBQ seitan, until I flipped the container on my lap by accident and BLAM, see ya! Have you ever watched snap peas fly in slow motion? It's not cute. Dag.

Papa is sad. Him and Mama tell me that it's okay to feel a range of emotions. Everyone does. Thing is, I've never seen Papa like this.

It may sound bugged, but it's nice to know that he's not a robot.

Papa has feelings just like I do.

We decide to see if other parks have their rims down, too. First, we visit Bed Stuy's "Soul in The Hole," where "Booger" Smith used to skate through multiple defenders then hit "Hammer" with the no look alley for two, all to the "oohs" and "aahs" of the crowd.

Then we drop by "The Hole" in Brownsville, which produced "Fly" Williams, World B. Free, and "Pearl" Washington aka "Pac Man," all of whom impacted b-ball's style of play as we know it today. Lastly, we hit up Tillary Park, where future NBA Hall of Fame inductee Bernard King dominated before he broke scoring records for the NY Knicks.

Papa has told me about these legendary parks and players so many times, I can finish his sentences for him!

My favorite tale is of "Sudden" Sam Worthen, who once played for the Chicago Bulls. Sam was at West 4th St., with hundreds of onlookers peering through the chain link fence. While dribbling, he spun on the man checking him, then did a half-spin, and then spun a third time, completely losing his defender, and…his shoe!

Sam scored the layup in his socks,
then sprinted back to pick up his sneaker.
Legend has it that his kicks were still spinning in a circle, ha!

The rims were down on every court we went to, which was fine with me. I didn't have to get anxious about my shot, meanwhile we explored the wonderful folklore of NYC playground basketball culture.

Mama suggested that me and Papa stay at home for a few weeks, so Papa went old school and grabbed a wire hanger. He formed a circle with it, placed it on the top of my bedroom door, then passed me a tennis ball and BOOM!

Now I play ball every night after dinner. Well, that is...after I've digested my food, ha, but if I had it my way, I'd wash my dish and go straight to backwards two-hand dunking. Wouldn't you?

In the early years of the sport, not everyone played with official equipment. In the first game ever played on December 21, 1891, the game's inventor Dr. James Naismith had his students shoot a soccer ball on a peach basket!

I hope Dr. Naismith emptied out all the fruit first. Could the sport have been called sticky peach ball had he not? Hmmm...

In the 1920s, European immigrants in Manhattan's Lower East Side loved the game so much, they crunched up newspapers and bound them with rubber bands, then used the bottom of a tenement building's fire escape ladder as their goal.

Eventually the city built more outdoor courts throughout the boroughs, and that's how the sport grew.

I still see kids my age shooting jumpers on the sidewalk. Some use an empty trash can as their goal; others ball on a hollowed milk crate hanging from a lamppost.

I first met Theophilus, Ireyna and Mamushi at our schoolyard's jungle gym. They were aiming their ball at an open square on the monkey bars! It looked like too much fun, so I asked if I could join. Mamushi and I were on the same team. He'd just moved from Japan and didn't speak English yet. Meanwhile, I had no idea what I was doing!

Didn't matter. The language of ball is universal.

We've all been friends since.

Mama doesn't pay much mind to basketball at all, but I've even seen her try to shoot a crumpled-up paper into her wastebasket while writing letters to family.

One time, I surprised her by blocking her shot! I punched it too hard, though, and her make-believe ball flew into Papa's mouth.

He was taking a nap with his lips open, trying to catch flies. Le whoops!

The WNBA season starts tonight! Papa puts on a game between the Chicago Sky and Dallas Wings for us. Before tip-off, I come up with an idea. "Papa, can I keep score?"

Mama and Papa are unschooling me, which allows me to explore whatever my interests are, and I...LOVE...MATH!

I need to review the rules. For any shots behind the three-point line, I add that amount for the team that made the attempt. Inside that line, the addend is two points.

FREE THROW = 1 POINT
FIELD GOAL = 2 POINTS
THE ARC = 3 POINTS

If a player gets fouled in the act of shooting, the referee awards them free throws, each of which are only worth one point. I think I got it.

The buzzer sounds.

Let's go!

"Papa, this is fun!" The pace is up-tempo with full court passes leading to fastbreaks, so I use tally marks instead of numerals to keep up.

Mama asks, "What's the score?" Hmm, okay. I can easily see groups of five thanks to my tally marks. Dallas has 5 + 5 + 5 + 5 + 5 + 2, so the sum is 27. Wait. Chicago has four groups of five plus one, so I can use multiplication first and then addition. (5 x 4) + 1 = 21. "27 to 21, Mama, with Dallas in the lead."

Papa asks, "How much is Chicago down by?" If I subtract 21 away from 27, the difference is six. "Six, Papa."

"How many threes would they need to tie the game?"

Hmm, okay. If I divide six by three, or break six into three parts, the quotient is…"Two."

And just as I say that a player shoots, but the ball doesn't reach the rim, or even the backboard. They look like me every time I shoot on a 10-foot basket!

A heckler in the front row yells out, "Airball!" so loud, I feel like they're in our living room and eyeing my last chocolate protein bar. Chill.

"Papa, should I minus a point because the player missed completely?"

"Nah! When we play 21 and someone shoots an airball when taking a free throw, they go all the way back to zero. In organized ball, though, there's no penalty for missing a shot. A team can only move forward in points, so long as all its players keep trying."

It would be fun to keep score using negative integers to move backwards on the number line, but I can dig it.

"Pa'lante, siempre pa'lante!" the Young Lords Party used to shout while fighting for social justice in the early '70s. It means "Forward, always forward."

"Mama, did you teach the Young Lords about having a growth mindset, too?"

"No baby… I wasn't born yet! You better fix your mouth thinking I'm that old, HA!"

The weather has gotten warmer lately, and it's wonderful to take long walks through the Brooklyn Botanic Garden to bird watch and explore nature.

There are a variety of trees to gaze at, like the native cherries, maples, and oaks. My favorite of all is the southern magnolia because of its fragrant and flowering qualities. When it's baking outside, I find shade under the branches to cool down.

I'll never forget the first time I saw a cardinal. I'm serious. The red of its feathers was so brilliant, I was able to spot him on a low hanging leaf-filled tree branch. He let me inch closer and closer until I was only a few feet away, then, whoosh! The stout bill pointed towards the clouds, and the scarlet wings propelled the songbird in the same direction.

The experience was nothing short of poetic.

Papa knows I observe my surroundings with a keen eye, so he takes me to the El Shabazz courts to combine my love for math with his passion for b-ball.

"Taína, how many circles can you find on this full court?"

Hmmm...if there were rims up, there'd be two of them. There's one circle at the half court line, and there's a circle around each of the two free throw lines. Altogether, that's 2 + 1 + 2. "Five circles, Papa."

"What about the ball that Theophilus is dribbling? Why didn't you include it?"

"A b-ball is not a circle, Papa. It's a sphere! A circle is a flat shape, whereas a sphere is a round object in space. That's why you can bounce it! Good try at tricking me, though, ha!"

"Excelente! Now take out your sketch pad, think creatively, and draw two more circular shapes, only using lines from the court."

Hmmm...this one is tough!

If I could look down at the court from above like a red-tailed hawk, I might have a better overview.

Let's see...I must use my imagination. Ah!

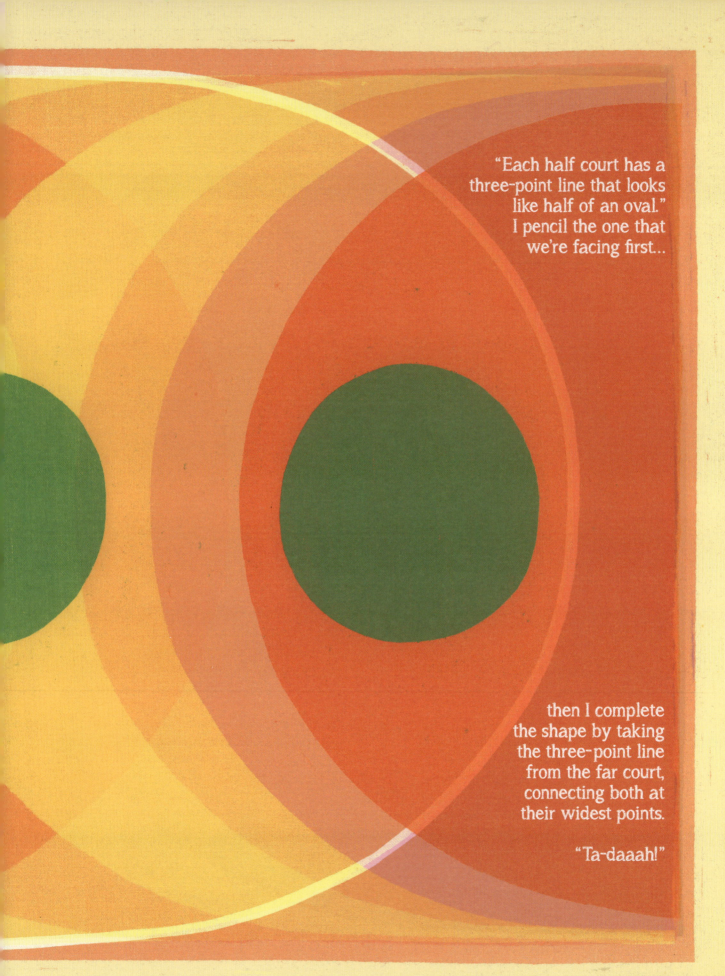

"Each half court has a three-point line that looks like half of an oval." I pencil the one that we're facing first...

then I complete the shape by taking the three-point line from the far court, connecting both at their widest points.

"Ta-daaah!"

"You rock! That's one, now stretch your mind and sketch one more circular shape. It's totally fine if you don't get it. Have fun either way."

Wow. I have to really put my brain cap on and eat some blueberries for this one! Okay, let's give it a shot...

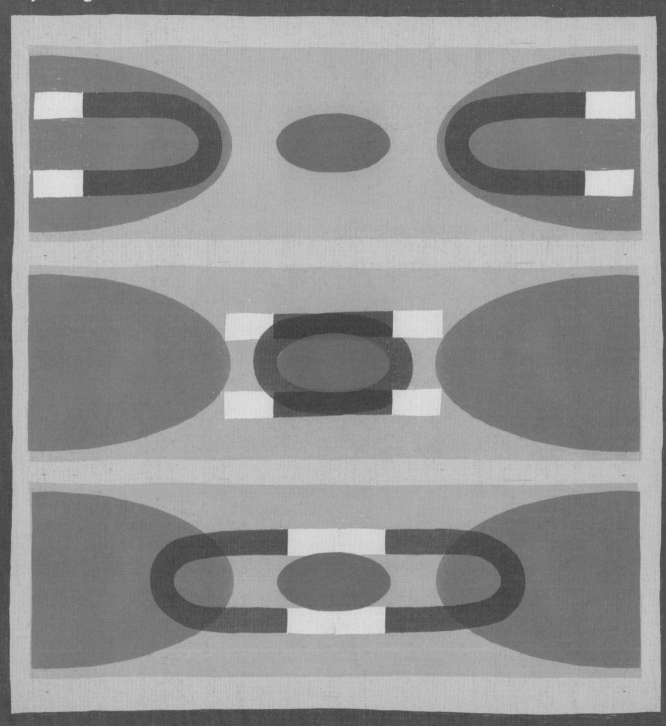

Papa loves to shoot while directly facing the backboard, because he thinks there's a magnet attracting his jumper into the rim. I told him magnets only attract iron, and that his ball didn't contain any metal. Wait. I got it...

"I see the shape of two magnets pointing in opposite directions on the free throw lanes of each court, Papa! Connect them at their open ends and boom."

"Bong bong! Two semicircles connected by two parallel lines is a shape named an arena. I only learned that myself last night while googling, ha!"

"How many triangles can you find?"

"I don't see any!"

"You don't see any..."

"Yet."

And as that word comes out my mouth, a blue jay flies overhead, which draws my attention to the reinforcement wires that hold up the backboard.

Two triangles on each side, two on the top, and two on the bottom.
(2 x 2) + (2 + 2) = 8.

"16 triangles, Papa. Eight on this basket and eight on the other side of the court."

"Last question: If the rims were up, what three-dimensional shape would the net remind you of?"

Theophilus knows the answer as well from the clinics, so we answer in unison, "An ice cream cone! Put the ball in the hole and what do you get? Two scoops!"

"You sound hungry! Let's go home and eat. Maaaybe we'll have dessert."

Papa loves to cook for me, and I greatly appreciate that but...his meals are like his three-pointers from NBA range. As in, 50% are money in the bank, and...50% of them are a miss! He doesn't follow recipes, and he's probably dreaming about basketball when he's adding the ingredients, so you just never know what the plate will taste like.

Mama on the other hand? She shoots 99%! As in 99 out of 100 meals taste bananas. Tonight, she's making coconut rice, black eyed peas, collard greens and for dessert? Sweet cornbread! Whaaat? Yum 3x, now let the horns blow "De neh neh deh deh neh!"

Mama joins us at the table and asks, "Taína, what are you grateful for today?"

"Well, I really like being homeschooled, but I don't know why it's called that! I learn just as much at the park. I am thankful for you and Papa supporting my passions. I am learning who I am in the process."

"That's called self-determination, where we as a people are allowed to define ourselves. It's a core principle of our African-American heritage."

"That reminds me of Kwanzaa! My favorite day was Imani, which means faith in Swahili. I really believe that tomorrow is going to be an incredible day."

Papa butts in, "And it will be, Taína. Putting hopeful thoughts in the universe attracts positive energy. Change can happen when we visualize its potential."

"I also have faith that I'll eat the last of the sweet cornbread, yaaaaaah!"

"Cute. Real cute. But you're not slick, yo!"

"Taína, catch!" Baba Kyle shouts as he shoots a mango my way while wearing an Indiana Fever WNBA jersey I don't recognize.

"Look up Tamika Catchings, a legendary player who was hearing impaired. She didn't let her disability hold her back, though, and she still wound up in the Hall of Fame as one of the greatest ever. Very inspiring story!"

"Gracias, Baba Kyle! Will do. Peeeace!"

It's been months since the rims came down, but that hasn't stopped Papa from practicing his jumper daily. He just uses the box on the backboard as his target, which has maintained his joy. I grew an inch recently, and now wonder, "Can I finally hit a jumper on a 10-foot rim?"

"Papa, can I climb that tree while you practice?"

"Of course! You don't even have to play ball—*at all.* I want you to be your own person. So long as you're expanding your horizons and having fun, I'm good!"

"I love you, Papa."

"I love you, too."

Just as Papa says those words, a pick-up truck drives and parks right in front of the backboard. Two Parks & Recreation Department workers open the cargo bed door, revealing a toolbox, a ladder, and...a rim.

Papa drops his ball. His hands are trembling. He can't contain his joy. I can feel his glee bouncing off my body the same way the sun rays are kissing my skin.

"Papa, can I ask them if I can help?"

I love to build things. Doesn't matter whether it's science experiments or coding. I think of my hands as a gift. They help me shape the world around me.

"That job can be dangerous, Taína, so best if done by adults. I tell you what, though. Once the rim is back up, if you'd like, you can take the first shot."

"But Papa, I can't even put the ball in the hole!"

"You can't put the ball in the hole..."

"I know. I know. I can't put the ball in the hole–yet."

"And you won't know..."

"...unless I try!"

The workers tighten the final nut and bolt. The rectangular backboard looks like the canvas from my art class to me now. I'm imagining the rim as a halo, or a sculpture to be appreciated at a museum.

I'm not the only one in awe. People from the neighborhood are excitedly gathering on the court. Papa passes me the ball.

I look up at the rim, and for some reason, it feels higher than it ever was before.

I'm nervous.

I feel so embarrassed. I just want to run. I want to climb up that tree and hide inside the branches.

One of the park workers says, "You were so close! Try it again. You can do it, girl!"

I haven't decided that I am a girl yet. Mama said that's okay, that in fact, I don't have to ever decide on being a girl or a boy. I can be either, both, or neither. I'm allowed to define myself when I'm ready. It's called self-determination.

I respond to the worker, "Thank you for the encouragement."

I want to try again.

All of a sudden, I spot Ireyna in the crowd. I haven't seen her since the rims came down. She steps forward and shouts, "Aim high, little giant. Aim high!"

Deep breath in. I can hear Mama in my head saying, "You have a growth mindset, Taína."

Deep breath out. I can hear Papa in my head saying, "Things can potentially change when we visualize that they will."

No more "I can't reach the rim yet."

"I can reach the rim." Right now.

"We're going to start today's clinic with geography. Mamushi, what Asian country is Tiger Asics from? Malaysia, the United Arab Emirates, or Japan?"

"Japan!"

"Theophilus, what European country are Puma and adidas from? France, Germany, or Spain?"

"Germany!"

"Ireyna, what North American country are Nike, New Balance and Converse from?"

"This is cute and all, but when are we going to play?!"

"Guard up, Ireyna! Let's gooooooooooooooo!!!"

Photo by Claribel Báez

Author Bobbito García is an NYC native who has put an indelible footprint on multiple urban movements.

As the progenitor of sneaker journalism, García penned his landmark *Source* article "Confessions of a Sneaker Addict" in 1990, then in 2003 became the critically acclaimed author of *Where'd You Get Those? NYC's Sneaker Culture: 1960-1987* (Testify Books). In 2005, ESPN's "It's The Shoes" series, hosted by Bobbito, became the first show on the subject in broadcasting history.

A former professional basketball player in Puerto Rico, García performed in the groundbreaking Nike "Freestyle" commercial. In 2007, the brand released seven co-designed Air Force 1 sneakers bearing his name. The voice of EA Sports' popular NBA Street video game is also a world-renowned DJ, who has spun World, Soul and Jazz music at Lincoln Center, Central Park SummerStage, and the Smithsonian (DC).

As an award-winning filmmaker, García has directed *Doin' It In The Park: Pick-Up Basketball, NYC* (PBS, NETFLIX), *Stretch and Bobbito: Radio That Changed Lives* (SHOWTIME, NETFLIX), and NY Times "Critics' Pick" *Rock Rubber 45s* (Smithsonian African American Film Festival 2018 official selection). Transitioning to TV, he also directed eight "SneakerCenter" episodes for ESPN+.

A founding member of the Kennedy Center's Hip Hop Culture Council and a 2018 Wesleyan University "Distinguished Alumni Award" recipient, "Kool Bob Love" currently produces his b-ball tournament Full Court 21 in four continents, co-produces music for the Stretch and Bobbito + The M19s Band, and co-hosts "Stretch and Bobbito Radio" on Apple Music Hits.

A self-proclaimed "outdoor b-ball activist," Bobbito has played in 48 countries and has acted as an ambassador for the sport, coaching clinics and donating sneakers in collaboration with various brands as well as non-profit organizations.

Bobbito currently lives in New York with his co-parent and their son, who cherishes being unschooled (and hasn't caught the bug to play basketball…yet)!

www.koolboblove.com

Photo by Daniela Nutz

Estefanía Rivera Cortés. Visual Artist.
"I do a lot of things."

Estefanía Rivera Cortés' artistic journey began when she was six years old. She couldn't stop drawing! Her first-grade teacher recognized her talent and gave her a key role to play in the classroom. Each time they studied new words, Estefania would create visuals on the chalkboard.

Since then, this artist based in San Juan, Puerto Rico has been self-expressing through performance art, visual narration, painting, and printmaking. Estefanía is passionate about using drawing as a form of meditative mind-body practice. She feels that this is one of the most intimate ways to connect with her creative energy.

As a Visual Artist with compassion for social causes, Estefanía is driven to create impactful imagery. Her mastery of visual storytelling has led to several empathetic illustrative works that have been featured in the Museum of Contemporary Art of Puerto Rico, the Clemente Soto Velez Cultural and Education Center, and the *Puerto Rico Review Magazine*.

www.estefaniariveracortes.com

GLOSSARY

B-ball: The sport of basketball, or the actual ball that is used to play with.

Crib: Where someone lives, as in home. Can be an apartment or house.

Biddy Rims: A basketball goal that is set lower than the standard height of 10 feet and used generally by children ages 10 and under to learn.

Negative Ups: Someone who may have difficulty jumping high or well.

As-salamu 'alaikum: An Arabic greeting which means, "Peace to you."

Wa-'alaikum as-salaam: An Arabic response to the greeting of "As-salamu'alaikum" which means, "And peace unto you."

The Iron: Another word for the rim on a backboard.

The Hole: Another word for the rim on a backboard.

A Rock: The ball that is used to play basketball with.

Bugged: Unintentionally weird or off.

Skate: Dribbling a basketball with extreme skill in between multiple defenders.

No Look Alley For Two: A pass that is made without looking at a teammate which leads to a dunk worth two points.

Unschooling: A form of homeschooling where children learn based on their interests rather than a set curriculum.

21/Utah: A game with no teammates or teams. The player with the ball attempts to score against all other participants on the court.

El Shabazz Playground: A place in Bed-Stuy, Brooklyn named after civil rights leader El-Hajj Malik el-Shabazz, also known as Malcolm X.

Kwanzaa: An annual celebration of African-American culture and values.

AGRADECIMIENTOS:

My Mummy, Sydney Shaw, Langston, Brother Ray, "Titi Julissa" Vale, Rob Hernandez @ B-ball Junkies, Ivan Rivera & Khrysti Hill + Chad Benson @ WeAreLittleGiants, Manolo Rivera, Estefanía Rivera Cortés, Baba Austin, Mr. Henry, Rosie Perez, Ramon Rodriguez, Ben Snyder, Dana James @ Testify, Seth Rosenfeld, Janine Bell + Aya Shakti & Zahra, Judy Pryor-Ramirez & Fernando Ruíz Lorenzo + Diego, Claribel Báez & Jessie Matias + Adrián & Elias, Elsie Aldahondo & Henry Maldonado + Evan, Vaughn Caldon + Simmy, Roman Perez + Leia, Amber Batchelor @ Ladies Who Hoop, Chiené Jones @ Grow Our Game, Zahra Habib, Monifa Giamanco aka Queen Searifa, Xochitl Gonzalez, Omar Acosta, Anne Marie Boidock, Rick Telander, Alex Wolff, Jesse Washington, Michelle Willems and Tio Chilly E!